MW01204474

Porous Land

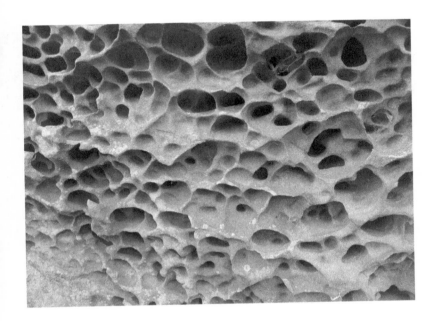

Poems by Agnes Vojta

Spartan Press

Kansas City   Missouri

Spartan Press
Kansas City, MO
spartanpresskc@gmail.com

Spartan
Press

Design, edits and layout: Jeanette Powers, Jason Ryberg
Cover and title page images: Agnes Vojta
Author photo: Thomas Vojta

I am grateful to all who supported and encouraged me during the journey that led to this book.

I owe a debt of gratitude to Jeanette Powers for their attentive reading and thoughtful suggestions for revisions. I thank Sophia Vojta for being a steady source of encouragement and good ideas, KC Dolan for sending me feedback even while traveling in New Zealand, and Cyndi McMillan for helping with *Seaglass*. Thank you, Jason Ryberg, for making this book possible. Thanks, Greg Story, for all the pep talks in your office.

I thank the editors of *Southwinds* and *The Gasconade Review* where some of these poems first appeared.

To my parents, Heidi and Hans Petzold, I am grateful for surrounding me with poetry and music as a child.

And always, thanks to Thomas Vojta for his steady support, patience, and love.

CONTENTS

For Thomas, Sophia, and Philipp

We shall not cease from exploration
And the end of all our exploring
Will be to arrive where we started
And know the place for the first time.

-T. S. Eliot

Silhouettes

Like dancers,
       the elms lift their arms
           skyward.

The oaks clutch the air
       with gnarled fingers,
bony branches
       etched into the pastel evening.

It is time
  to step forward,
      uncloaked,
naked shadows
    dancing
       on the canvas of the world.

How to Make Paper

Tear paragraphs limb from limb,
    shred sentences,
        blend words to a pulp—
all alchemy begins with destruction.

Water catalyzes the transformation.
Pour,
    gently
        lift the embryonic sheet
          out of its bath,
smooth its wrinkled skin,
press the fibers into holy matrimony.

Then wait—
    reincarnation requires patience.

Rough around the edges,
infused with memories,
the new paper
bears faint traces
of former wisdom.

River Song

I call to the ageless river
who does not justify her existence
but just flows:

Green river,
    speak to me.

Green river,
    teach me
        to turn obstacles
           into song.
Green river,
    sing to me, let
        your many voices
         take root
           in my heart.

Journey

We set out a long time ago.
Years stretched before us, a vast land,
with pathways and hills to explore.
We journeyed.

Too soon,
we are nearing the shore of the sea
where you will embark
on a ship to a country I cannot
see in my dreams.

Sure-footed,
you will step aboard
and perhaps glance backwards once.

I shall remain on the shore,
sand slipping through my hands.

I Watch You Sail Away

on the blue stream of the years,
uncharted
current and tides,
different than they were
on my voyage.

My tattered maps
will be of no use to you,

but I gave you
my compass—
this has to be
enough.

Deserted

A bleak morning, I waken
    to relentless rain.
        Drops pearl the redbuds.

Broken branches beckon
    with oily fingers.

A deserted nest perches
    in the plum tree;
        black and wet, it does not
           remember the fledglings.

Snowless

Gray waves of oak trees roll
over the hills until they melt
into a gray horizon.

A dogwood tree lies cut,
its swollen buds
an unfulfilled promise.

The willows have wept
lancet leaves that sleep
in the creek, imprisoned in ice.

Behind pale palisades of reeds
the lonely pond reflects
the gray sky.

Vanishing Act

The stream disappears, swallowed
by insatiable karst. We live
on porous land.

Skin deep soil hides the unknown:
passages that worm through earth flesh
open into wombs and cathedrals.
Flowstone gleams wet like mucous membranes.

Water seeps through fractures,
dissolves and deposits.

We must descend deep
to understand
what lies below,
where crystals form
under heat and pressure.

Grown larger, the stream
emerges again down valley,
unexpected.

The Greening Begins from the Ground

not in the high places
that still belong to winter,
not on the barren ridges
where buzzards rest on bare branches,

but in the valleys
where shy white flowers
hide by the creeks
and green shoots
push through the soil.

Growth begins
in the humble hollows.

Prophecy

A gentle gurgling in the glades:
the rains have awoken
the waterfalls.
All the little valleys sing.

On the banks of the stream
witch hazel foretells
the coming of spring.

The Bluebells

We wandered
into the realm of the bluebells
that dwell in the flood plain
after the spring rains.

Carefully,
we stepped
through the blue kingdom.

We could not hear
the tiny bells
ringing with mirth,

but we saw
the great heron lift off
toward the river,
his silent blue winged shadow
gliding over the flowers.

The Magnolias Were Magnificent

a sea of pink promises
ready for bloom.

The freeze
withered
the petals.

But is this sadder
than never
to have budded
at all?

Sea Anemones Invaded the Cedars

After the April rain,
the cedars bear alien fruit:
gelatinous growth
like orange sea anemones,
slimy creatures whose
slippery tendrils quiver—
sporeful,
revolting and fascinating,
life
fills all niches.

Only One Morning

Spiderwort
before dawn—
a cluster of buds
waits
for the light:
one flower may waken.
Who chooses?

Three petals open,
cut from the summer sky,
which they mirror
until midday
when they tire,

fold,
return to the bud.
Green clasps shut;
within, petals melt
to drops of purple.

At nightfall
the sepals enfold
only the memory
of a flower.

Left

Light dances. The water is
liquid sky. The waves
long for the shore, the faint
line of the horizon
lost in the distance. Vast
like a sea, the great
lake lies, and I
left you there.

April Is Cruel

Angry waves assault
the shore, drench
the path we walk
each time before
I leave you
in the glistening city.

Today,
clouds shroud
the skyline, and goodbye
cuts with sharper edges.

The Spring Rains Were Relentless

The house struggles
to keep its roof
above water. The river
smashes it into trees; they
slash the walls,
slice the roof.
The house thrashes,
rips a telephone pole out by its root,
crashes;
boards swirl,
splinters in brown sludge.

The round eye
of the satellite dish
does not blink
before drowning.

Key Hole

Blue skies,
sunny
Zion
morning.
At two-
twenty,
weather
warning:
flash flood
danger!
Canyons
closed to
travel.

Hikers
deep in
Keyhole
Canyon
are now
out of
cell range.

Rain and
hail slam
out of
the black.

Water
pours down
steep rock
walls, falls
from all
cracks, whirls
logs, hurls
trees. Flood
crashes
through the
narrows.

Seven
bodies.

In memory of the hikers who died in Keyhole Canyon,
Zion National Park, 2015.

Chaparral

The land sizzles.
Brittle grass
yellows the hills.
Live oak draw
sparse circles of shade
over spiky shrubs.
Hot wind rustles.

The chaparral holds its breath,
waits for the spark.

Later,
in the ash covered ground,
seeds waken and stir.

Requiem for a Eucalyptus Grove

i. Ellwood Mesa, 1994

The green air tasted of mint. The dense
canopy dropped shade
into the hollow. A brown
rustle clustered the branches—
dead leaves, I thought, until

they fluttered orange: here was
the place where the butterflies gather,
ten thousand monarchs dreaming winter away
in an enchanted forest.

ii. Ellwood Mesa, 2017

A graveyard of trees
after merciless drought years—
peeled bark curls
at the skeletons' feet.
Shrill sunlight
hits the dust.

Pathless

The canyon maze
fractals
the landscape.
Self-similarity deceives.

Dry potholes burrow
in red rock. Salt
crusted rims smell like thirst.

Nobody dares
to say the word:
lost.

Without You

The house feels hollow,
the only sound: my footsteps.
You took the laughter with you.

Minutes drip slowly.
The specter of loneliness
stares at me with greedy eyes.

Therapy

As I walk in the woods,
the worries
melt off my shoulders.
My jaw softens.
My hands unclench,
unfurl
like the wings of the wild geese
that sculpt the wind.

Mountain Meditation

I hike in silence.
My feet follow
the rhythm of my breath
which is molded
on the contour of the mountain.

I think only
of breathing and walking,
breathing and walking
until I reach
the summit
and realize:
I spent the morning
in meditation,
every step
a prayer.

Pilgrimage

I surrender.
The labyrinth
weaves my way.

The path will lead me
to the center
if I just
let it happen.

Lesson

A white *S*
among the reeds,
the egret
can teach me
poise and patience.

Sea Glass

Your wholeness
broken, you became
a fragment.
Sharp edges speak of loss;
cuts leave scars.

Surrender
to the endless ocean.
Waves toss and roll;
sand grinds the wound,
slowly dulling the grief.

One day you emerge,
translucent,
smooth and beautiful,
frosted with wisdom.

Growth in an Old Garden

— After a painting by Paul Klee

Greedy green has devoured
its assigned space—
untamed
explosion of leaves, fronds, vines,
blades, briers, branches.

Trees tower over the old house.
Empty
windows stare.

Ferns fan mossy stones
below broken fountains.
Dim rhododendron rooms still
echo
with children's dreams.

Midsummer

The year is crowned
with a wreath of flowers.
Dreams stand in high bloom.

Dance around the fire in your soul
drunken with light,
your heartbeat the sacred drum,

the golden petals of the flame
flickering skyward.

July

Sunlight seeps
through the blinds,
oozes into the room.

The ceiling fan sweats
from its labor.
The clock creeps
at half speed,
pendulum dragging
through syrupy air.

Sluggish afternoon hours
stick
to our skin,
steep us
in lethargy.

Mt. Hope

The summit daunts.
Courage shrivels.
I must not look up.

Patiently
I string steps
on the thread of my breath,
and trust:
I will arrive.

From time to time,
I look backwards
to see how far
I have come.

Cleaning out Your Room

I sifted through years of memories
that ran like sand
through my hands.
A few treasures remained behind;
carefully,
I packed them away.

Afterwards,
I sat for a long time
and listened to the rain on the roof.
Through your window,
I saw a slate sky.

Revision

Revision is an exercise in humility.
We should perform it regularly,
like house cleaning:
question choices,
throw out junk,
discard the stale,
clean and polish.
Apply to poems and life.
Repeat.

Gathering Poems

I went into the woods
to seek solitude
and found poetry,
uncovered words
under old leaves and
decoded secret messages
in the pebbles by the stream.
The stones whispered to me,
and the silence
distilled into song.

Fabulous Friction,

your magic transforms
the steep rock into
footholds.

In delicate balance,
we dance on
invisible
stairs to the
summit.

Climbing Raven Rocks

I dance upwards;
below me,
the waves slap the cliffs
and beat the rhythm.

Wind-whipped clouds gallop
with flying manes
across the blue plain of the sky.

The wild geese resent
our intrusion.
Honking displeasure,
they swoop a warning: *you are guests here.*

The cedars smell
of summer and freedom.
I lean back
into the arms of the world.

Anointing

The Goddess dwells
in high places. Her green
mantle flows
over the slopes.
Her silver braids
cascade
like waterfalls.

I lie down
among rocks and grass
and feel her embrace,
and the waters of a mountain stream
anoint my brow.

Blessing on Highway O

Barkless, the withered
tree raises its arms
like the statue of an ancient
God, carved
by a forgotten people,
calling
a blessing on all
who pass.

Cathedral Woods

October sunlight streams
through stained glass windows—
mosaic of yellow and red.

Tree pillars
hold up the sky dome.
Wind organ whispers.

Orange flames,
sassafras and sumac
light the path
to the altar.

Comparing Autumn Leaves to Gold is Cliché

and feeble— when did gold ever shine
like this? Only
fire and passion flame
like the maples.

The trees dance a wild
celebration, shout in orange
exuberance, get drunk
on the last sunshine,
the fermented essence
of summer.

Ozark October
throws a crazy party at the edge
of darkness, and we are
invited.

Leaf Pondering Fall

As long as I can remember
I have been green and on this branch.
They tell me soon I will become tinged,
glow red,
burn orange,
or shine like gold.
I can hardly wait!

And soon after, I shall
embark on that journey
they have been talking about,
and I am a bit scared.
A wind will come, they say,
and rip me away,
fling me into the air,
whirl me around in mad dance,
toss me, smash me,
lash me
with rain
before I crash
to the ground
all wet and ripped,
they say.

But maybe, some say,
on a quiet sunny day,

a tiny breeze, almost unnoticed,
will gently pluck me off,
and I shall sail on the air,
swaying to and fro,
and descend softly
onto a rustling pile.

Einstein's Heirs

Two black holes spiraled
and merged. Their dance
sent ripples
through the universe.

Racing at speed of light,
waves warp
space -
time.

A billion years later,
on a small planet,
laser beams bounce
between mirrors,
capture the echo.

Einstein's heirs
decode
the message.

Traveling Light

Star born
photons,
unburdened by mass
hurtle
through vacuum voids.

On a green planet, a woman
looks up at the night sky.

The photons travel
through her eye
and die
on her retina.

Electric pulses race
along the optic nerve,
and her miraculous brain
translates:
I see a star.

Ephemeral

Frost flowers bloom at the feet
of white crownbeard, only
at the threshold of winter, before
the sap retreats to the roots.

The stalks exhale. Vapor
freezes to ribbons that curl
around pale stems
like bows of blown glass.

White in the morning grass,
the most fleeting of flowers
linger longest
in the deepest shade.

December

The last days
cling to the year
like late leaves
to the oak trees.

Every song
is a goodbye.

Time's tired steps
echo hollow
in the deserted birds' nests.

Destiny

Silver haired, the year
rests in the field.
Crows gather
on the sycamore bones.
The day tastes like glass.
Winter lurks
in the shadows.

In brittle glades
papery pods protect
the last seeds.
Empty coneflowers stand tall;
the goldfinches had their harvest—
everywhere signs of a cycle
fulfilled.

I Learn to Live with the Silence

Thoughts echo
in the empty house.

I transform your room
into my space,
place
candles and shells
on the windowsill.

Your books are still
on the shelves—
old friends
who keep me
company
and speak of you.

Full Circle

We have come
full circle.
We took out
the leaves
that extended our table.

The small round
seats
the two of us

like it did
twenty years ago.

Clarity

In the cold, all doubts condensed
and precipitated from the air, leaving
translucent winter light.
It is the hour of sharp contours.

The lake rests secure
in its stillness, twinning
the trees in precise reflection; even

the telephone wires appear
drafted in black stylus
on the water.

Wasp Nest

This is what it means to be
queen:
to emerge alone
from the dark
and to start
building an empire, relying
only on yourself;

to wait in solitude,
giving food, protection,
the warmth of your body,
until your first subjects
crawl from their cells, ready to
feed, fortify and defend;

to withdraw
into the inner chambers of your
pale paper palace
and do what only
the queen can do: be
the life-giving mother of your tribe;

to die
at the end of your one year reign,
survived
by a dozen daughters,
your deserted fortress
decaying in the wind.

Milkweed

The capsule burst open.
Fuzzy floss spills out—
soft white parachutes
for small seeds that yearn
to float away like dreams.

Coloring Inside the Lines

Coloring books are a refuge
from a world
where choices have consequences.

They provide direction
with just the right amount of freedom
and no correct solution in the back.

Limited options soothe
the decision fatigued:
cerulean or indigo— what
does it matter?

Luxury

I shall splurge
on a box
of black
pencils—
pointy promises that hold
treasures of words.
The rubber end
erases my mistakes,
a luxury
life does not
afford us.

Infinity

The exquisite pleasure
  of being the first
    to step on freshly fallen snow:

untouched

the field spreads,
  a white infinity
    of possibilities.

Oracle

The heron is the color
of a November morning.
Fog wets the river rocks.
Fossils faintly echo
a gray past.

I shall take one stone
home,
to look
through its waterworn hole
and see
the future.

Agnes Vojta grew up in Germany, spent a few years in California, Oregon, and England, and now lives in Rolla, Missouri where she teaches physics at Missouri S&T. Her work has been published in *The Gasconade Review, Poetry Quarterly, Southwinds,* and elsewhere.

This project was made possible, in part, by generous support from the Osage Arts Community.

Osage Arts Community provides temporary time, space and support for the creation of new artistic works in a retreat format, serving creative people of all kinds — visual artists, composers, poets, fiction and nonfiction writers. Located on a 152-acre farm in an isolated rural mountainside setting in Central Missouri and bordered by ¾ of a mile of the Gasconade River, OAC provides residencies to those working alone, as well as welcoming collaborative teams, offering living space and workspace in a country environment to emerging and mid-career artists. For more information, visit us at www.osageac.org

Osage Arts Community

CPSIA information can be obtained
at www.ICGtesting.com
Printed in the USA
BVHW031518150421
605031BV00009B/770

9 781950 380015